Fun Kitchen Collectibles

Jan
Lindenberger

Schiffer Publishing Ltd

77 Lower Valley Road, Atglen, PA 19310

Acknowledgements

I wish to thank Lori L. Murray, the owner of The Antique Merchants Mall in downtown Colorado Springs, Colorado, for allowing me to photograph her extensive kitchen collection. Lori's help in arranging and rearranging was greatly appreciated. The Mall's specialty is kitchen collectibles of all eras. Her personality and love for this collectible made it a pleasure to do this book in her shop. And many thanks to Courtney McWilliams and Doug Hastings for their assistance.

Also thanks to the following, and anyone else I may have missed:
Adobe Walls Antique Mall, Colorado Springs, Colorado
Yesteryear Antiques, Upper Lake, California
Antique Merchants, Colorado Springs, Colorado
Colorado Antique Gallery of Littleton, Littleton, Colorado

Copyright © 1996 by Jan Lindenberger

All rights reserved. No part of this work may be reproduced or used in any form or by any means--graphic, electronic, or mechanical, including photocopying or information storage and retrieval systems--without written permission from the copyright holder.

Printed in China

ISBN: 0-7643-0022-9

Book Design by Michael William Potts

Library of Congress
Cataloging-in-Publication Data

Lindenberger, Jan
    Fun kitchen collectibles/ Jan
    Lindenberger.
        p.   cm.
    ISBN 0-7643-0022-9 (pbk.)
    1. Kitchen utensils--Collectors and
collecting.   I. Title.
TX656.L56   1996
683'.82'075--dc20   96-18764
                                         CIP

Published by Schiffer Publishing, Ltd.
77 Lower Valley Road
Atglen, PA 19310
Please write for a free catalog.
This book may be purchased from the publisher.
Please include $2.95 postage.
Try your bookstore first.

We are interested in hearing from authors
with book ideas on related subjects.

Contents

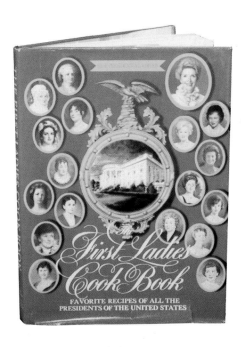

Kitchen Collectibles

Since this is the era for bringing back the old, collectors and decorators are in their glory. Plastics have made a strong comeback and now there is a revived interest in the old metal, tin, glass and iron kitchen items, dating from the 1890s to the 1970s.

One does not need much of an imagination to decorate with these wonderful objects, or to realize the usefulness of them. From the old metal can openers to wooden spoons, from food strainers to the old glass refrigerator jars the variety of kitchen tools and implements is inexhaustible. Even electric toasters and mixers have been revived

Clever collectors find new uses for old objects. What a homey feeling one gets when seeing the wooden butter bowls used for holding fruit or displaying flowers. Tin fruit strainers make colorful planters also. And sometimes the old use is the best.Tin bread boxes kept the bread fresh for days and are still being used. Tin and ceramic canister sets and cookie jars are as useful today as in the beginning. Metal whips and egg beaters are kept in the wooden hoosiers ready to be used. And used they are. The metal and tin kitchenware was virtually indestructible.

Kitchens have always had useful devices and gadgets in them. In 1889, the J.Ingalls Co. advertised for "lady agents to sell a unique article called the nutmeg grater." This item sold for 25 cents. It was about that time that the name gadget caught on.

Spice sets came in a variety of sizes and shapes, as did salt and pepper sets. From figural plastic, glass, or metal to jar-like sets or advertising pieces. Many of theses colorful pieces were sold not only at the "5 and 10 cent store," but also at souvenir shops. Spice sets were made in many sizes and with a combination of different spices. Often vinegar and oil sets were included with the spice sets.

Juice reamers, too, came in many sizes, shapes and materials, including glass, tin, aluminum, sterling silver, iron, wood and metal. Some were electric, and many were hand held. This useful tool gave the user fresh juice in a short time, but it was a messy job.

Wooden mallets, meat pounders, butter bowls and paddles, butter churns, rolling pins were the least expensive of the kitchen implements, so most of the homes had these much needed and used implements. Because of their durability, many of these wooden tools have survived to appear in antiques dealers shops today.

Iron pots and pans and utensils were in kitchens in the 1930s. They never seemed to wear out. By the late 30s colorful wooden handled utensils, such as egg beaters, whips, beaters, and mashers replaced much of the tin and iron.

Mixing spoons, spatulas, strainer spoons, skimmers, slotted spoons came in a variety of sizes and shapes and were the housewive's special tools. These utensils found extensive use. The strainer spoon and skimmer could skim off grease from any soup and lift the vegetables out of the broth. Spatulas lifted food out of the cast iron pans with ease and the mixing spoons usually had wooden handles for safety. How many times have you found a wooden handle spoon with a burnt handle? To me burn marks gives the spoon character.

According to Linda Campbell Franklin, author of *300 Years of Kitchen Collectibles,* the first recipes were hand written and passed from generation to generation. Some terms used in early cook books were inexact, like "pinch of salt," "dab of butter," "shake of baking powder" or "a squeeze" or "dib of this" or "a dab of that." Amazingly enough the recipe usually came out right. We have come a long way...and aren't we thankful?

Hopefully, this book on popular kitchen collectibles, will give the collector and buyer an overall perspective for this collectible. I hope you enjoy this information and price guide and take this much needed book with you while you are on your hunting trip for kitchen collectibles.

The prices may vary according to geographical area, condition and availability. Shop prices may differ from flea market prices or auction prices.

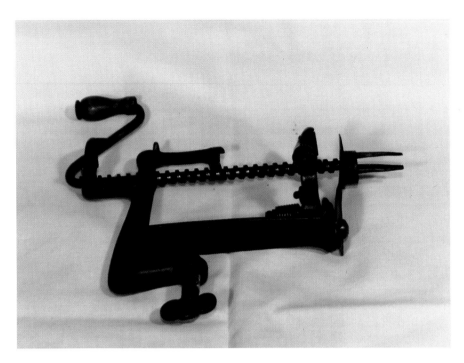

Iron apple peeler. 1890s. $65-90

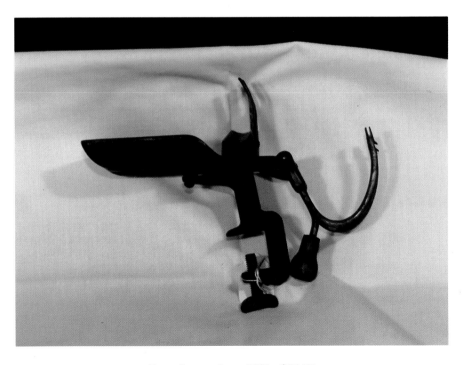

Iron cherry pitter. 1890s. $55-75

Iron cherry pitter from New Bright, Pa. 1890s. $80-100

Iron apple peeler from Goodell. 1890s. $85-100

Iron apple peeler from Reading Hardware. 1890s. $85-100

Plastic "Krisk" bean stringer and slicer. 1960s. $10-14

Jar opener with plastic handle. 1930s. $7-10

Garlic press from Ekco. 1940s. $5-7

Aluminum pie crimper. 1940s. $6-8

Aluminum cheese slicer. 1940s. $15-20

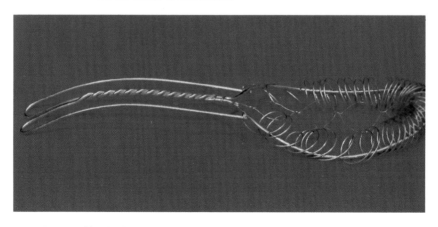

Wire egg/food whip. 1940s-50s. $4-6

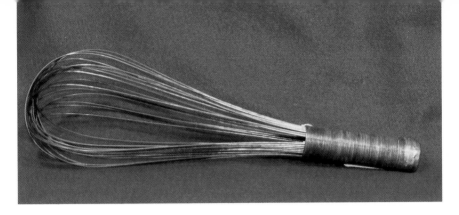

Wire food whip. 1940s-50s. $7-10

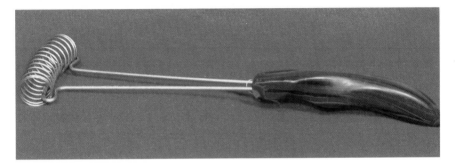

Wire whisk with wood handle. 1950s. $5-7

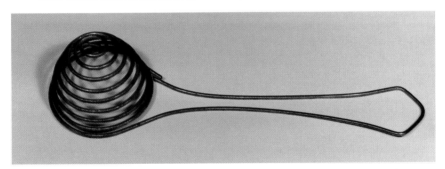

Wire whip 1930s. $8-12

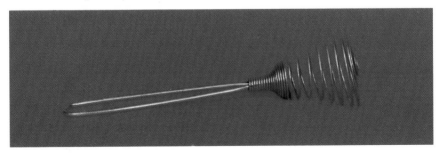

Wire whip. 1940s-50s. $4-5

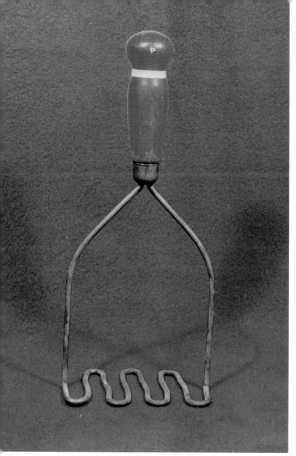

Wood handle masher. 1950s. $5-7

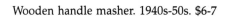
Wooden handle masher. 1940s-50s. $6-7

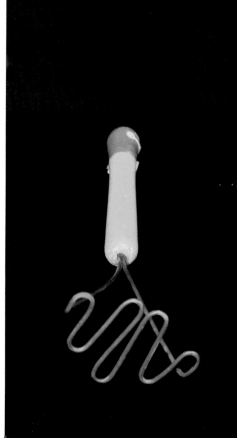

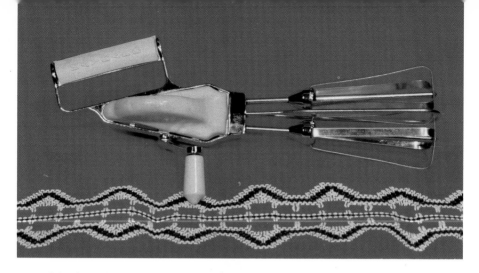

Metal egg beater with plastic handle. 1960s. $12-18

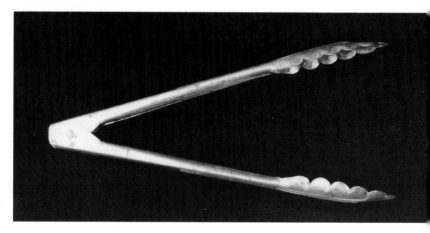

Metal sandwich toaster/hamburger
maker by Nut Brown. 1970s. $7-10

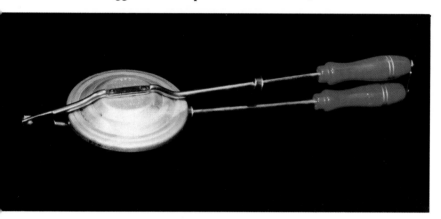

Metal ice or salad tongs. 1940s-50s. $2-3

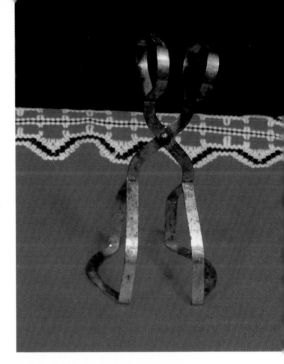

Metal jar lifter. 1930s. $7-10

Metal bottle/jar opener. 1940s-50s. $10-15

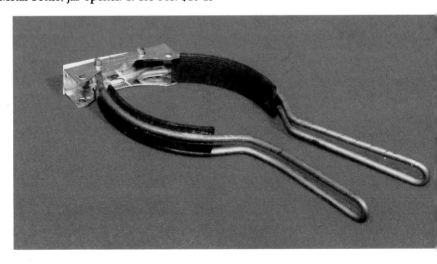

Metal jar lifter. 1930s-40s. $6-10

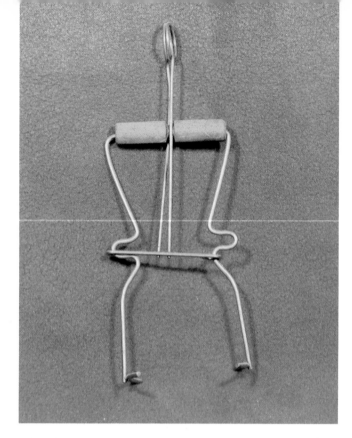

Metal jar lifter. 1940s. $7-10

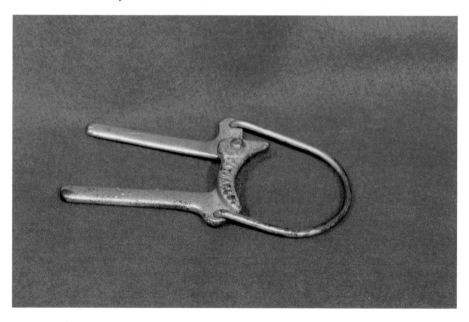

Metal jar opener. 1930s. $10-15

Metal jar opener. 1940s-50s. $4-5

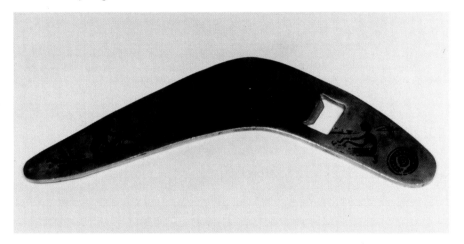

Metal boomerang bottle opener. 1950s. $15-20

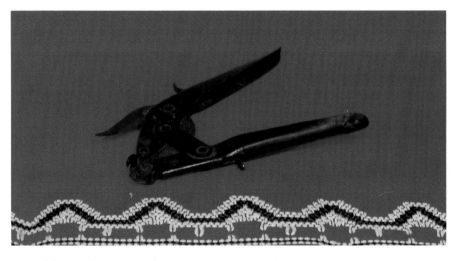

Metal military can and bottle opener. 1930s. $20-25

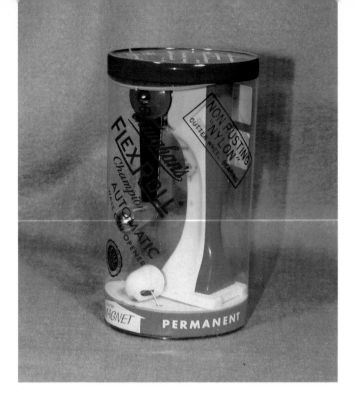

Magnetic can opener. 1960s. $30-40

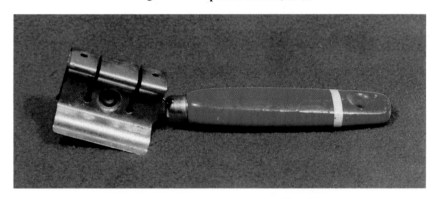

Wood handle knife sharpener. 1950s. $5-7

Wood handle cork screw. Screws into wood handle for safety. 1940s. $8-10

Plastic handle ice cream scoop. 1940s-50s. $30-40

Aluminum ice cream scoop with bakelite handle. 1940s. $10-15

Metal ice cream scoop by Nuroll. 1940s. $15-20

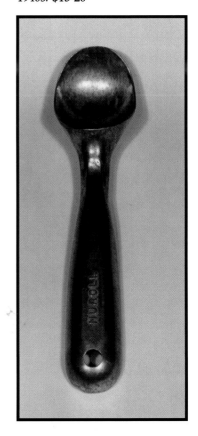

Metal ice cream scoop by Zeroll. 1940s. $20-30

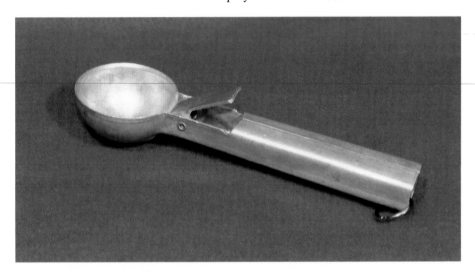

Aluminum ice cream scoop. 1960s. $10-15

Metal ice cream scoop with lever. 1940s. $10-15

Aluminum measuring spoons. 1960s.
$6-10

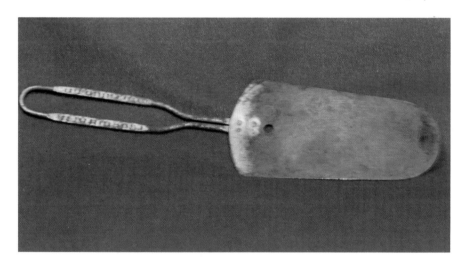

Advertising pie/cake lifter. 1940s. $5-7

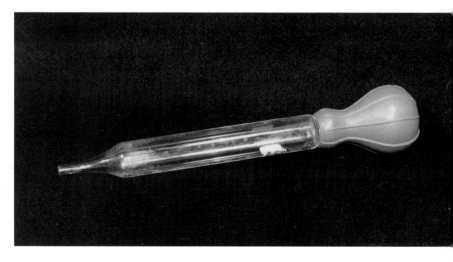

Glass baster by Purex. 1960s. $5-7

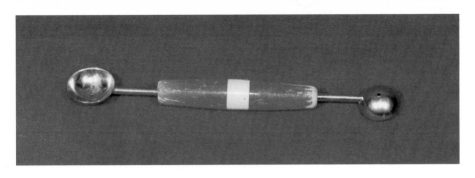

Metal melon baller. 1940s-50s. $2-3

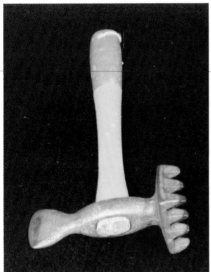

Wooden handle meat pounder/
tenderizer. 1940s-50s. $7-9

Wooden handle metal french fry cutter.
1950s. $5-7

Metal egg cooker. Eggs sit on inner rim and the rack is immersed in boiling water to the level marked for soft-medium-hard level. 1930s. $20-25

Wire egg holder. 1940s. $25-30

Plastic donut maker by Popeil. 1950s. $10-14

Coppertone cake carrier. 1950s. $15-20

Metal cake carrier. 1950s. $8-12

Metal cookie canister with bow design. 1940s-50s. $7-10

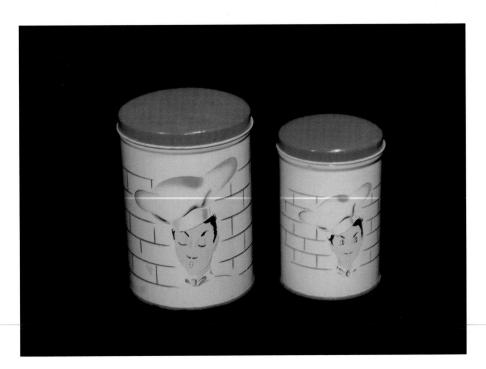

Metal chef canister set. 1950s. $5-6

Metal canister set with red lids. 1950s. $4-6

Metal floral design canister set. 1950s-60s. $18-25

Metal canister set with floral lace-look lids. 1950s-60s. $20-30

Silhouette metal canister set. 1930s-40s.
$20-30

Metal cracker design canister set. 1950s. $20-30 set

Red plastic canister set. 1950s. $30-40

Metal cookie tin. 1940s. $15-20

Metal basket with wood handles. 1950s. $25-35

Metal bread box with blueberry motif. 1940s. $10-15

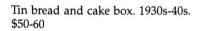

Tin bread and cake box. 1930s-40s. $50-60

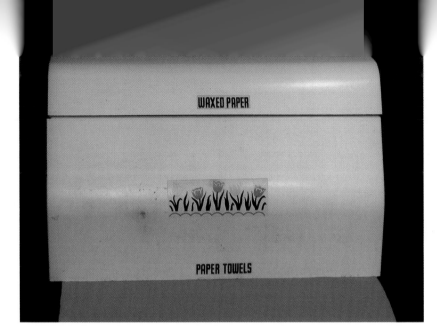

Metal wax paper and paper towel
dispenser. 1950s. $7-10

Plastic advertising jar for Lifesavers
candy. 1970s. $12-15

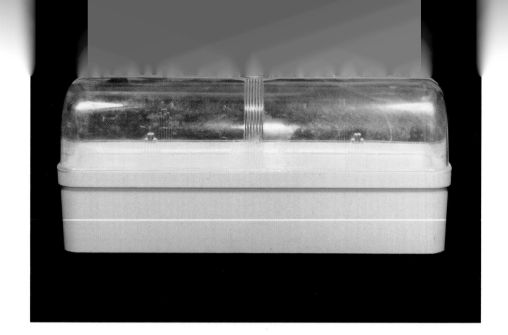

Plastic bread keeper. 1940s-50s. $12-18

Plastic ice bucket. 1950s. $20-25

Plastic ice bucket. 1950s. $15-20

Milk glass floral batter bowl. 1960s. $20-25

Green depression glass four-cup measure. 1930s. $35-45

Clear glass two-quart measuring/ batter bowl. 1960s. 15-20

Green USA pottery pitcher. 1930s. $30-40

Pottery molasses jug. 1930s. $100-125

Glass jars with decals. 1940s-50s. $5-8 each

Glass "Orange-Crush" juice jar with wood lid. 1960s. $35-45

Glass carafe wrapped in plastic trim. 1960s. $6-8

Satin glass syrup server. 1950s. $20-30

Glass syrup servers. 1950s-60s. $12-20

Clear glass syrup servers with plastic tops. 1950s. $6-10

Clear glass syrup servers with plastic tops. 1950s. $6-10

Glass syrup servers with plastic tops. $6-10

Glass syrup server with metal handle. 1960s. $6-10

Glass refrigerator juice jar. 1960s. $15-20

Glass refrigerator juice jar. 1960s. $6-10

Glass refrigerator dish with cover. 1950s. $10-15

Plastic Kool-Ade pitcher and cups. 1960s. $10-15 set

Insulated "Pelican Cooler."
1950s. $15-20

Glass food chopper. 1960s. $8-12

Glass food chopper/measuring cup. $8-12

Glass nutmeg/nut chopper with metal lid. 1950s. $7-10

Bulb-type jar nut chopper. 1940s. $10-15

Glass nut chopper. 1940s. $10-15

Glass nut/nutmeg grater. 1950s. $12-18

Glass jar nut chopper. 1950s. $10-15

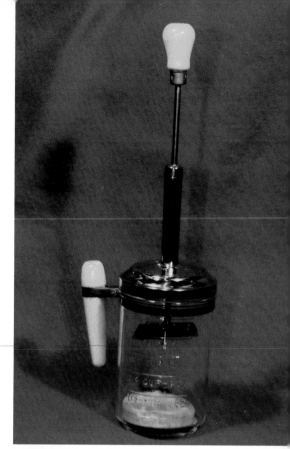

Glass mixer jar/mayonnaise maker.
1940s. $30-40

Glass mixer jar with wooden paddles. 1920s-30s. $45-55

Metal food chopper/vegetable crimper. 1940s. $4-6

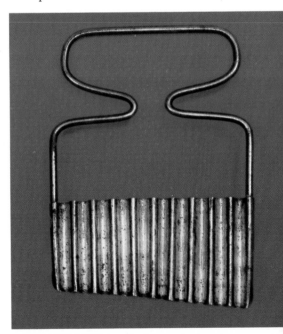

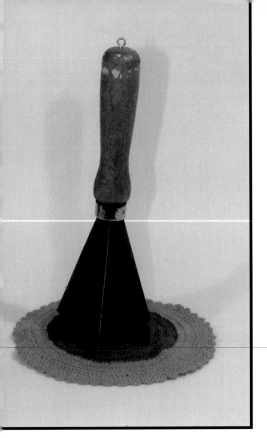

Metal food chopper with wood handle. 1930s. $15-20

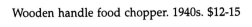

Wooden handle food chopper. 1940s. $12-15

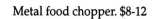

Metal food chopper. $8-12

Meat cleaver. 1940s. $7-10

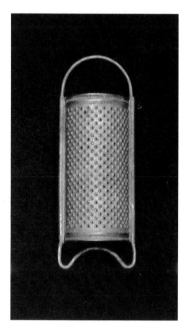

Metal nutmeg grater. 1940s-50s. $5-7

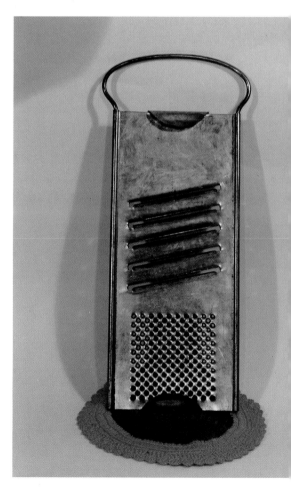

Metal with wood handle nutmeg grater. 1940s. $15-20

Metal food grater. 1940s. $4-5

Metal food graters by Super. 1940s-50s. $3-4 each

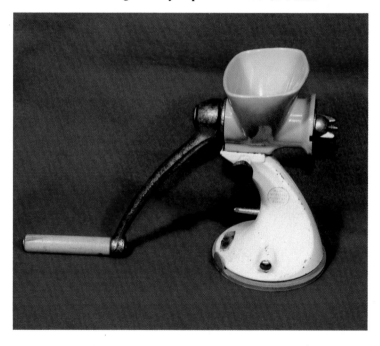

Porcelain meat grinder. 1930s. $30-40

Meat grinder by Enterprise. 1930s-40s. $20-30

Meat grinder by Keen Cutter. 1940s. $30-40

Meat grinder by Steinfeld. 1904. $35-45

Ice crusher, green enamel. 1940s. $20-30

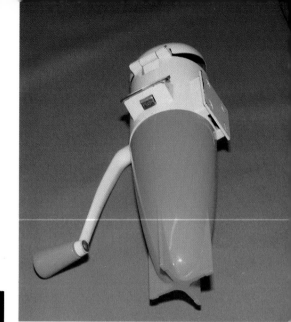

Aluminum strainer. 1940s. $3-5

Aluminum food strainer/
skimmer. 1940s. $5-7

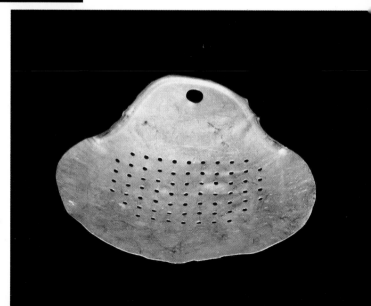

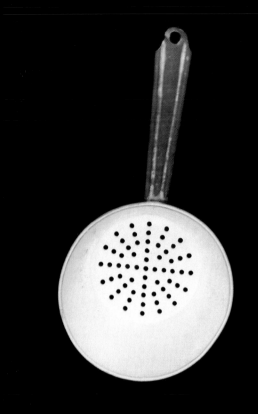

Aluminum food strainer. 1940s. $3-5

Wire strainer with wood handle. 1950s. $6-8

Metal food strainer. 1960s. $6-8

Aluminum food strainer. 1950s-60s. $5-7

Tin strainers. 1940s. $5-8 each

Tin food strainer. 1940s. $8-10

Tin sieve with handles. 1930s. $6-8

Tin grease screen. 1940s. $8-10

Metal flour sifter. 1950s. $10-15

Tin flour sifter/measure by Prize. 1930s-40s. $12-15

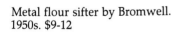

Metal flour sifter by Bromwell. 1950s. $9-12

Metal one cup sifter. 1950s. $8-10

Plastic flour sifter by Popeil Bros. 1940s-50s. $7-10

Metal flour sifter. 1950s. $15-20

Two-cup metal flour sifter. 1940s-50s. $6-8

Metal sieve with wooden masher and wooden handle. 1920s-30s. $15-20

Cone shaped aluminum strainer on metal stand. $12-18

Tea strainer. 1960s. $5-6

Metal tea strainer. 1970s. $4-5

Tea strainer and bag holder. 1910. $30-40

Metal tea strainer. Fits over tea cup. 1940s. $15-20

Metal strainers with wood handles. 1950s-60s. $5-7 each

Wood handle strainer. 1950s. $7-10

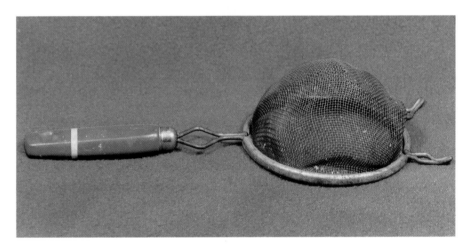

Wood handle strainer. 1950s. $6-8

Metal food grinder with wooden handles. 1940s. $15-20

Plastic reamer. 1950s. $10-14

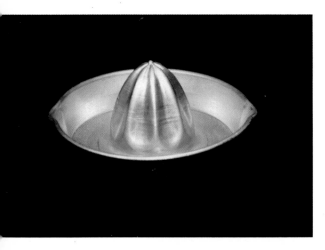

Aluminum citrus juicer. 1940s. $3-5

Aluminum citrus reamer by Kwicky. 1940s. $6-8

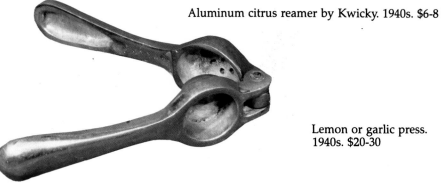

Lemon or garlic press.
1940s. $20-30

Plastic reamer. 1950s. $6-8

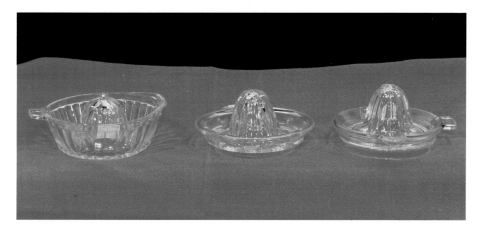

Clear glass citrus reamers. 1950s. $7-12 each

Metal hand ricers. 1940s. $10-15 each

Ceramic melon head men salt and pepper set. Japan. 1940s. $12-16

Ceramic dogs salt and pepper set. 1940s. Japan. $6-9

Ceramic salt and pepper heads. 1960s. $10-15

China poodles in a basket salt and pepper set. 1940s. $15-20

Ceramic fuzzy peaches salt and pepper set in basket. 1970s. $9-12

Glass polka dot salt and pepper set. 1940s-50s. $25-30

Glass sugar and creamer set. 1950s. $8-12

Glass salt and pepper barn set. 1960s. $7-10

Ceramic tomato salt and pepper set. 1940s. $15-20

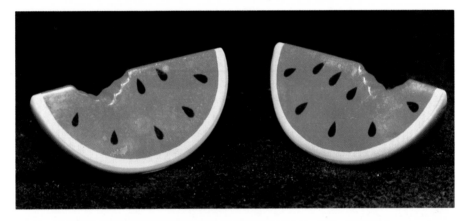

Ceramic watermelon salt and pepper set. 1950s. $30-40

Ceramic salt and pepper set with natives on cauliflower. 1940s. $50-60

Chalk salt and pepper set. 1940s. $40-50

Ceramic children salt and pepper set. 1980s. $35-45

Chalk chef salt and pepper set.
1940s. $40-50

Ceramic Mammy and Chef salt and pepper set. 1950s. $35-45

Ceramic chef and cook salt and pepper set. 1950s. 40-50

Milk glass salt and pepper set with aluminum lids. 1940s-50s. $25-30

Plastic hanging teapot with salt and pepper set. 1950s. $12-17

Plastic salt and pepper set. Toaster and toast. 1950s. $8-10

Plastic salt and pepper set, mammy and chef. 1950s. $45-55

Plastic salt and pepper set. 1950s. $7-10

Plastic salt and pepper set. 1950s. $6-8

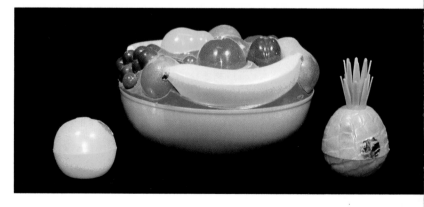

Plastic fruit salt and pepper set. 1960s. $15-20

Plastic egg-shaped salt and pepper set. 1960s. $8-12

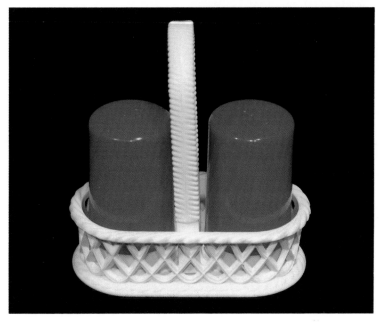

Plastic salt and pepper set in plastic basket. 1950s. $5-6

Wall hanging plastic apple salt and pepper. 1960s. $20-25

Plastic salt and pepper set. 1950s. $15-20

Wooden salt and pepper set in holder. 1940s. $12-16

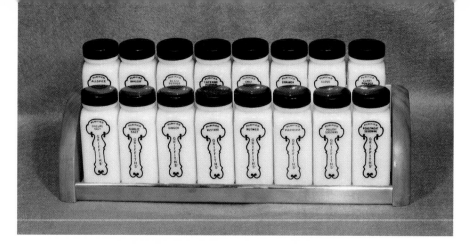

Griffith spice set in wooden rack. 1950s-60s. $40-50

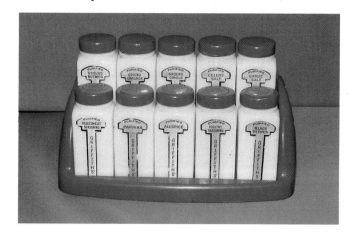

Griffith plastic spice set. 1950s. $20-30

Milk glass spice set in tin holder. 1940s. $25-30

Ceramic spice set in wire holder. 1960s.
$20-30

Ceramic spice set on rotating base.
1950s. $30-40

Ceramic spice set in wood holder.
1960s. $20-30

Chef spice set. 1950s. $80-100

Aluminum spice set. 1950s. $20-30

Tin holder with five spices. 1950s. $10-15

Plastic spice rack. 1950s. $25-30

Ceramic cow creamer, sugar, salt and pepper. "Japan." 1950s. $30-40 set

Plastic condiment set. 1950s-60s. $20-30

Green depression glass oil and vinegar set. 1940s. $40-50

Condiment set with spoons. Glass jars with plastic holder and lids. 1950s. $18-24

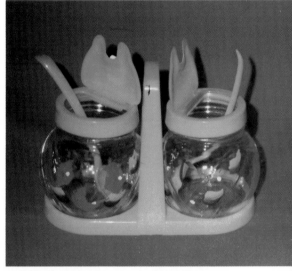

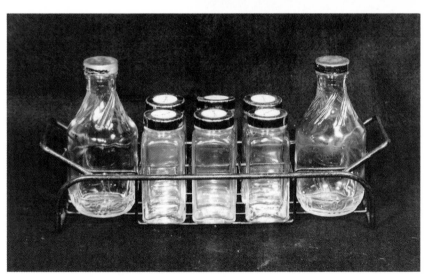

Clear glass spice set in rack by Griffith. $80-100

Ceramic apple, jelly or jam jar. 1970s. $7-10

Ceramic jam jars. 1960s. Japan. $6-10 each

Ceramic jam jars from Japan. 1960s. $6-10 each

Clear glass sugar shaker with plastic spout. 1960s. $8-12

Satin glass sugar shaker with metal top. 1950s. $25-30

Glass vinegar and oil set wrapped in plastic trim. 1960s. $6-10

Satin glass bitters bottle with cork
stopper. 1950s-60s. $6-10

Glass coffee jar. 1950s. $6-10

Ceramic cheese shaker. 1950s. $15-20

Clear glass salt jar. 1940s. $40-50

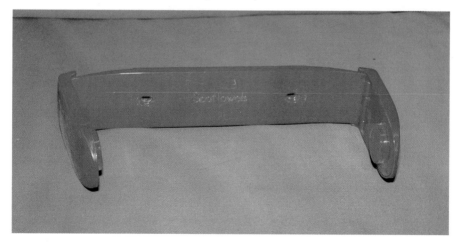

Plastic paper towel holder. 1960s. $8-12

Aunt Chick's plastic cookie cutters. 1940s. $30-35

Crumb catcher. 1950s. $10-14

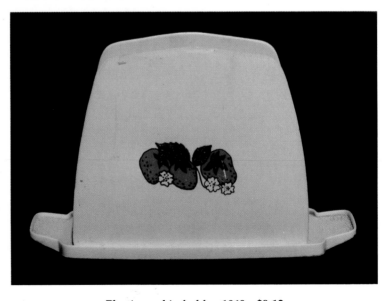

Plastic napkin holder. 1960s. $8-12

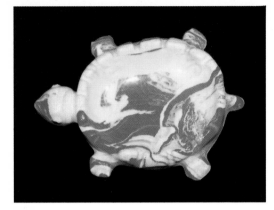

Plastic soap/Brillo pad holder. 1960s. $5-7

Plastic napkin holder with floral design. 1950s-60s. $8-12

Plastic straw holder from Lego, Japan. 1960s. $15-20

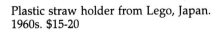

Metal green silverware holder. 1930s.
$7-10

Plastic clothes sprinkler with cork
plug. 1930s. $20-30

Clothes sprinkler. Plastic by Lustro Ware. 1950s. $6-10

Plastic clothes sprinkler. 1950s. $7-10   Plastic clothes sprinkler. 1950s. $7-10

Plastic advertising scoop. 1950s. $4-6

Plastic egg whip.
1950s. $8-12

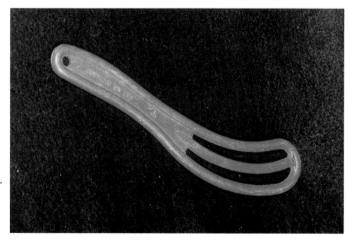

Plastic scales by House Proud. 1960s. $25-35

Plastic cookie jar by Burroughs Mfg. Co. 1950s-60s. $20-30

Plastic love birds spoon rest advertising Shurfine Foods by Admiration Plastics. 1960s. $7-10

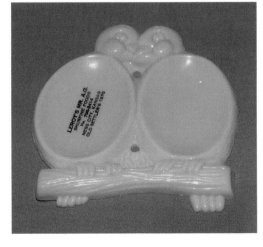

Plastic jello cups. 1960s. $5-6

Plastic butter dish by Plasmetl. 1950s. $12-16

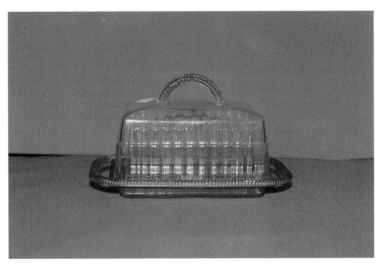

Plastic butter dish, advertising John Deere farm equipment. 1950s. $20-30

Plastic shopping reminder. Noma Happy Chef. 1950s. $15-20

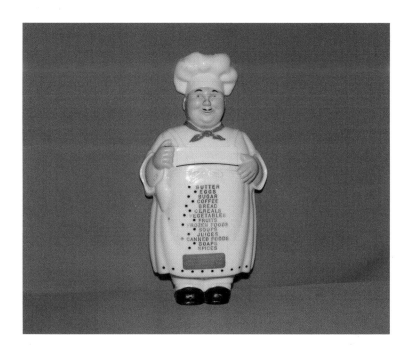

Plastic shopping reminder. Noma Happy Chef. 1950s. $15-20

Plastic wall pocket. 1950s. $8-12

Metal advertising teapot thermometer. 1960s. $10-15

Plastic note holder with chef holding paper. 1950s. $12-18

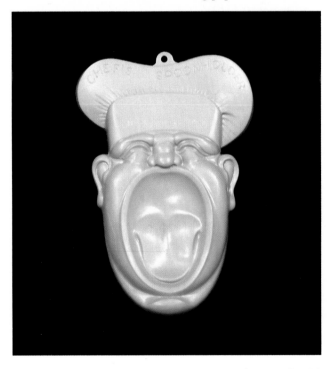

Plastic spoon rest with a wide-mouthed chef. 1950s. $15-20

Plastic juice pitcher. 1960s. $12-16

Plastic juice pitcher by Luster Ware. 1950s. $7-12

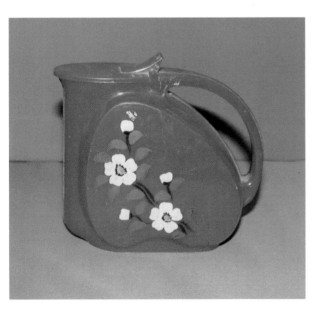

Plastic red floral juice pitcher, 1950s. $10-14

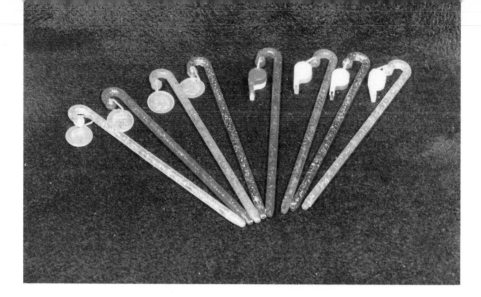

Plastic drink stirrers. 1940s. $10-15

Meat fork with Bakelite handle. 1940s. $5-7

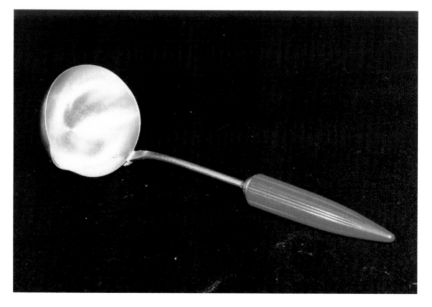

Aluminum soup ladle with Bakelite handle. 1960s. $6-8

Bakelite handle silverware sets. 1930s-40s. $20-30

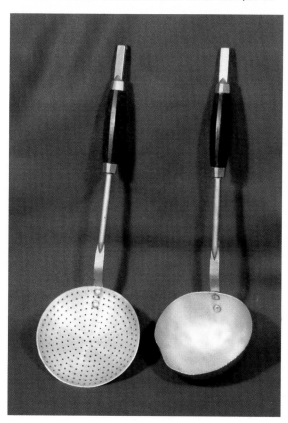

Pewter strainer and ladle set with wood handles. 1940s. $30-40 set

Plastic cow coffee creamer. 1950s-60s. $8-12

Wooden napkin holder. 1940s. $5-7

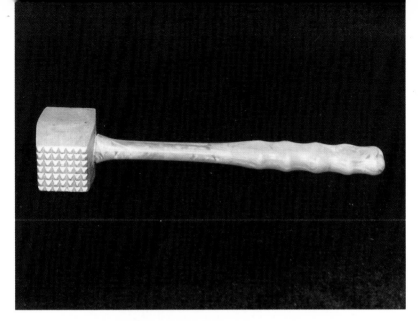

Plastic handle wooden meat pounder. 1950s. $4-5

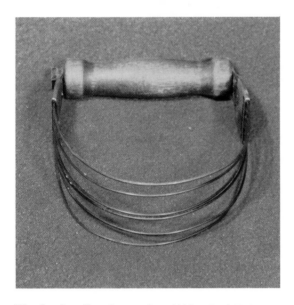

Wooden handle wire masher. 1930s-40s. $12-16

Wooden masher. 1940s. $10-15

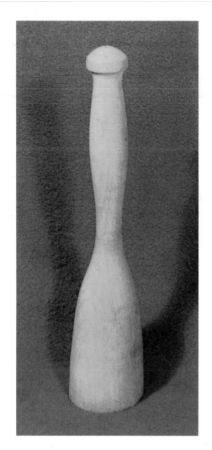

One piece wooden masher. 1930s-40s. $15-20

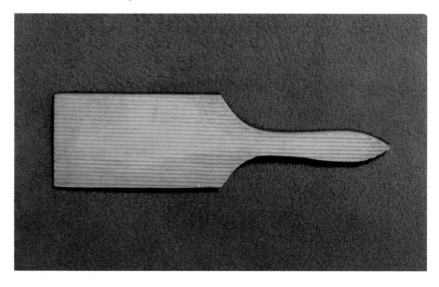

Wooden butter paddle. 1930s-40s. $10-15

Wooden butter paddles. 1930s-40s. $10-15 each

Wooden butter bowl with paddle. 1930s-40s. $50-60

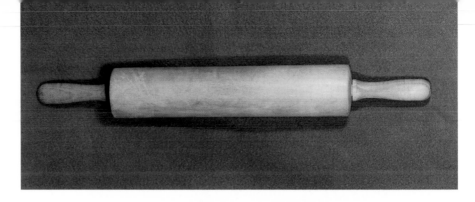

Wooden rolling pin. 1940s. $10-14

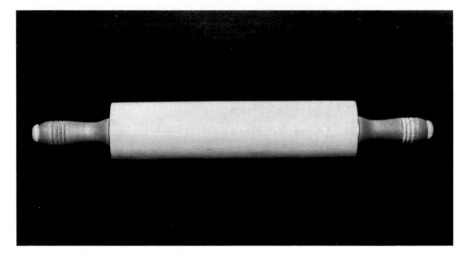

Wooden rolling pin with green detachable handles. 1940-50s. $10-15

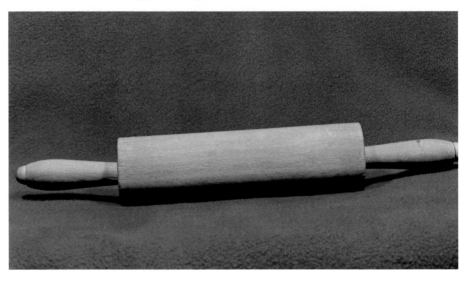

Wooden rolling pin. One piece. 1940s-50s. $15-20

Wooden rolling pin with red handles. 1940s-50s. $10-15

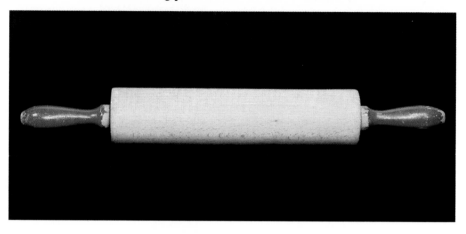

Wooden rolling pin with green handles. 1940s-50s. $10-15

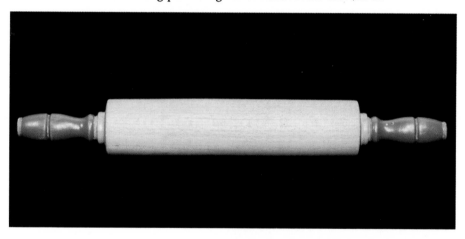

Wooden rolling pin with wide handles. 1940s. $15-20

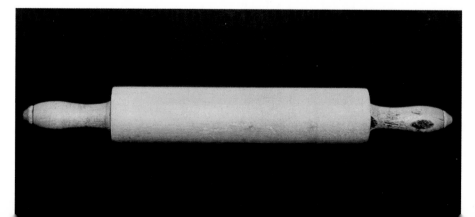

Wood slicer/dicer. 1950s. $15-20

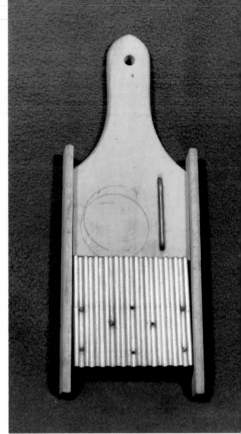

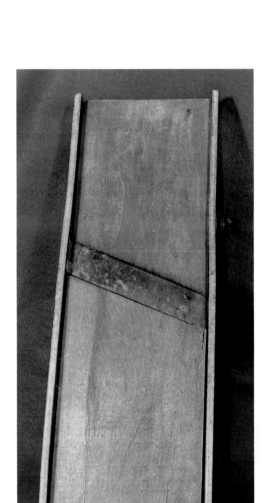

Wooden kraut cutter. 1920s-30s. $20-30

Aluminum funnel cake pan by Ovenex. 1930s-40s. $8-10

"Swans Down Cake Flour" advertising cake pan. 1950s. $20-25

Gray enamel muffin tin. 1930s. $20-30

Aluminum cake pan with lifter by Ovenex. 1940s-50s. $4-5

Aluminum cake spring form cake pan. $5-6

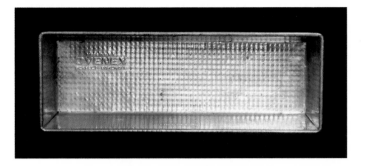

Oblong bread pan by Ovenex. 1950s. $5-7

Aluminum bread pan. 1940s. $3-4

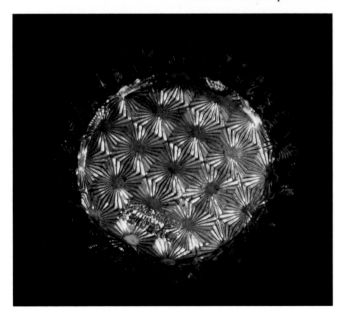

Fluted cake pan by Ovenex. 1950s. $6-8

Metal cake pan with "Ole Vir-gin-a" label. 1940s. $30-40

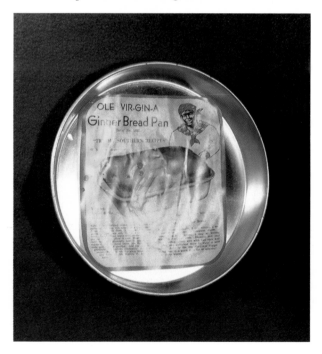

Metal cake pan with "Ole Vir-gin-a" label. 1940s. $30-40

Metal jello mold. 1940s. $15-20

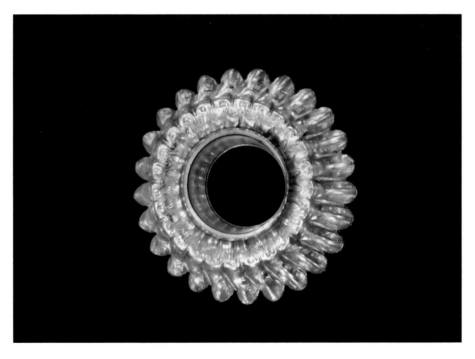

Metal fluted jello mold. 1940s-50s. $5-7

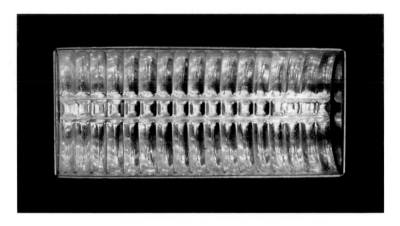

Metal German bread pan. 1940s. $6-8

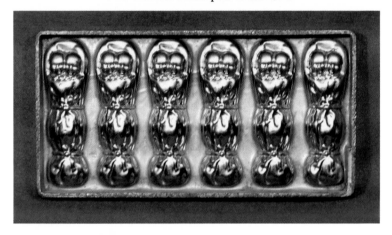

Candy mold of two babies wrapped in a blanket. 1930s. $25-35

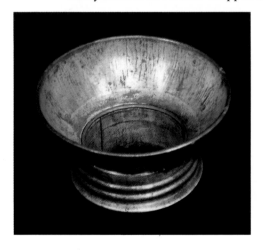

Tin funnel. 1940s. $6-8

Metal baker's mold. 1930s. $30-40

Tin pudding or jello mold. 1940s-50s. $20-30

Aluminum coffee pot. 1940s-50s.
$12-15

Aluminum coffee pot. 1940s-50s.
$15-20

Aluminum coffee pot. 1940s. $8-12

Silver on copper tea pot. 1930s. $20-30

Club aluminum coffee pot. 1930s. $15-20

Reed and Barton silver soldered pitcher. 1930s. $35-45

Chrome coffee pot with Bakelite handle. 1930s-40s. $30-40

Silver overlay coffee pot with wood handle. 1920s-30s. $30-40

Aluminum cooker strainer. 1930s. $35-45

Aluminum malt mixer by Thompson.
1940s. $15-20

Aluminum dispenser. 1930-40s. $20-25

Copper jello molds. 1960s. $3-4 each

Aluminum tooth pick holder. Shaped like a spittoon. 1950s. $6-8

Gray enamel funnel with loop handle. 1930s. $15-20

Gray enamel funnel. 1930s-40s. $14-18

Gray enamel strainer. 1930s-40s. $15-20

Gray enamel pan set. 1930s. $7-12 each

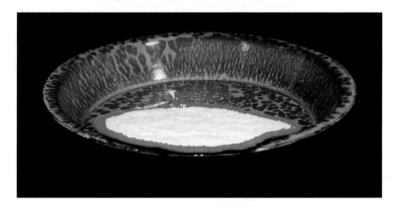

Gray enamel pie pan. 1930s. $8-12

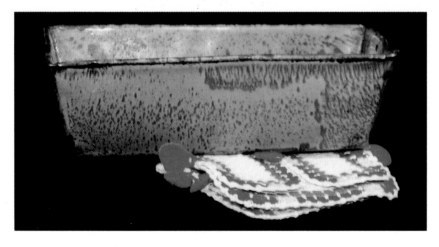

Gray enamel bread pan. 1930s. $15-20

Gray enamel bean pot with wire and wood handle. 1930s. $18-25

Gray enamel saucepan with lid. 1930s-40s. $15-20

Enamel ware lid with hook handle. 1930s-40s. $6-8

Metal muffin tin by Kreamer. 1940s. $12-18

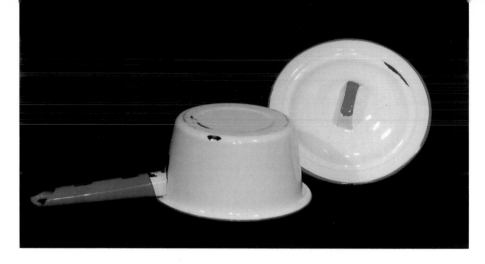

White enamel saucepan with lid. 1940s. $8-10

White enamel double boiler. 1940s. $10-15

White enamel colander
with red trim. 1930s.
$7-10

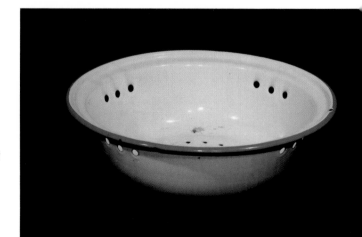

Enamel pans with red trim. 1940s. $5-7

White enamel coffee pot with red lid and handle. 1940s. $25-35

White enamel spaghetti pot with black trim. 1940s. $12-16

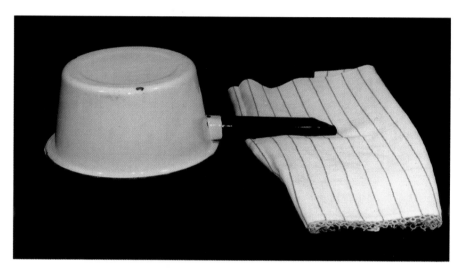

Enamel sauce pan with black trim. 1940s. $15-20

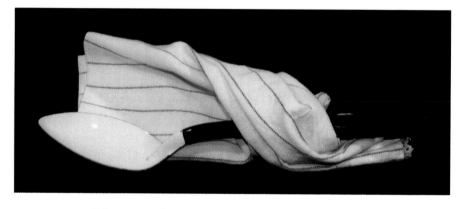

White enamel spoon with black handle. 1940s. $7-10

White enameled drinking cup. 1940s. $4-5

Enamel coffee pot. 1940s-50s. $30-40

White enamel tea pot with wire and wood handle. 1930s-40s. $20-30

White enamel coffee pot. 1930s-40s. $35-45

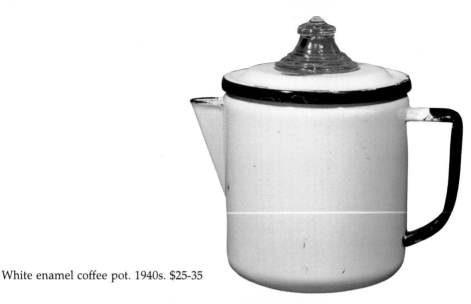

White enamel coffee pot. 1940s. $25-35

Enamel strainer on stand. 1940s. $15-20

Enamel drinking cup
with blue trim. 1930s. $4-6

Enamel bread box. 1940s. $75-100

Blue enamel strainer. 1940s. $10-14

Blue enamel double boiler. 1930s. $15-20

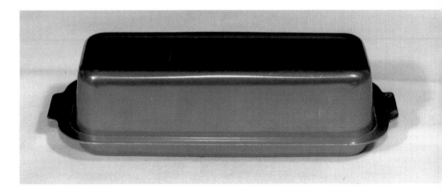

Aluminum butter dish. 1960s-70s. $7-9

Aluminum and glass salt and pepper set. 1960s-70s. $7-9

Aluminum grease jar. 1960s-70s. $12-16

Aluminum apple cookie jar. 1960s-70s. $25-35

Aluminum mugs with handles. 1960s-70s. $20-25 set

Aluminum juice pitcher. 1960s-70s. $15-20

Aluminum cream and sugar set. 1960s-70s. $8-12

Aluminum footed tumblers. 1960s-70s. $6-7 each

Aluminum tumblers. 1960s-70s. $30-40 set

Aluminum ice bucket. 1960s-70s. $10-15

Aluminum juice pitchers. 1960s-70s. $8-12

Aluminum sherbet dishes with glass inserts. 1960s-70s. $10-15 each

Aluminum coasters. 1960s-70s. $3-4 set

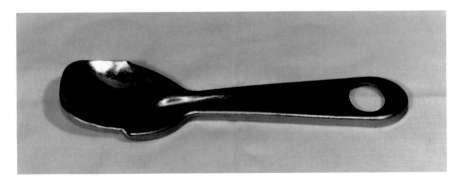

Aluminum shortening/ice cream scoop. 1960s-70s. $3-4

Aluminum tea pot with Bakelite handle. 1960s-70s. $15-20

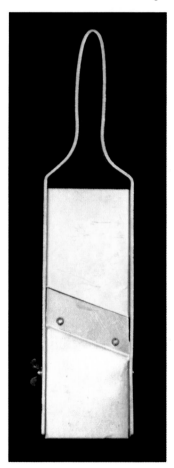

Aluminum slicer. 1940s. $6-8

Aluminum silent butler. 1960s. $9-14

Aluminum two tier tidbit tray. 1950s. $10-15

Club aluminum gravy bowl and tray. 1940s. $17-25

Dainty Dorothy's Cookie Molds. 1940s. $35-45

1914 electric toaster. $30-40

Electric two-slice toaster. 1930s-40s. $25-35

Chrome toaster. 1950s. $20-30

Electric chrome drip-a-lator.
1940s. $15-20

Electric pop corn popper. 1930s.
$20-30

Electric waffle iron. General Electric. $40-50

Electric mixer. 1950s. $15-20

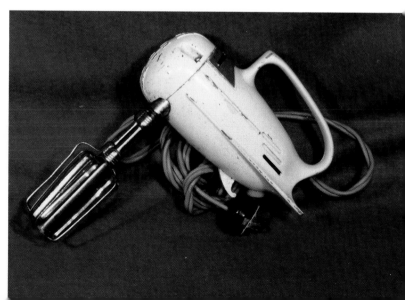

Electric mixer with green depression glass bowl. 1940s. $60-75

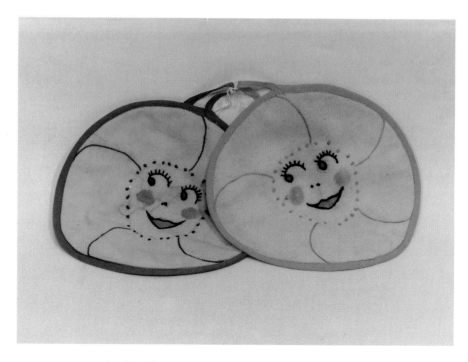

Smiling faces hot pot holders. 1950s-60s. $6-7 pair

Crocheted hot pot holders, vest shaped. 1950s-60s. $6-7

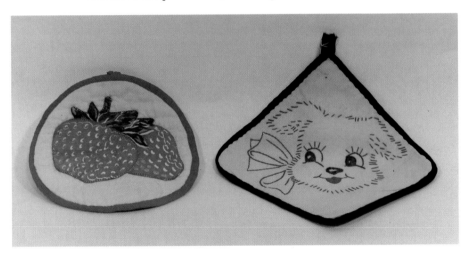

Cotton hot pot holders. 1950s-60s. $4-5

Crocheted hot pot holders. 1950s-60s. $4-5 each

Crocheted hot pot holder. 1950s. $4-5

Embroidered basket that holds two
butterfly pot holders. 1940s. $10-14

Cotton embroidered hot pot holder. 1950s-60s. $4-5

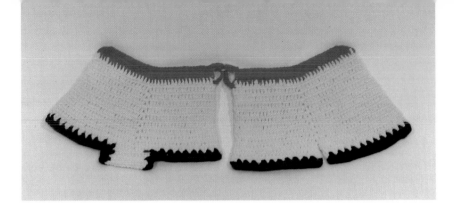

Chrocheted "undies" hot pot holders. 1950s-60s. $8-10 pair

Cotton fish and cat hot pot holders. 1950s. $4-6 each

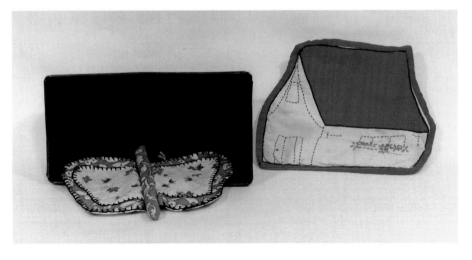

Cotton embroidered butterfly and house-shaped hot pot holders. 1950s. $3-5 each

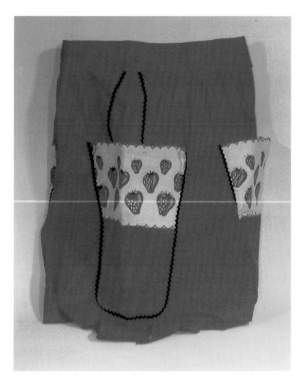

Red cotton strawberry trimmed apron. 1950s. $6-8

Red hearts and checkered cotton apron. 1950s. $7-10

Red apple checkered cotton apron. 1950s-60s. $8-12

Cotton floral apron trimmed in rick-rack. 1950s. $7-10

Cotton tea towels. 1950s. $4-7 each

Cotton printed tea towels. 1950s-60s. $5-8 each

Cotton printed table cloth. 1950s. $10-15

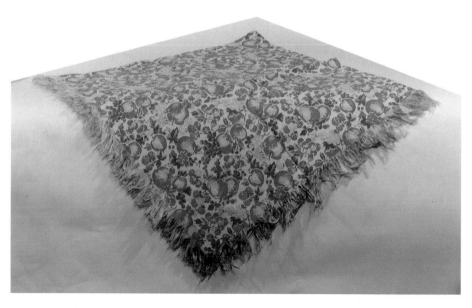

Cotton fruit print luncheon cloth with fringed edges. 1940s-50s. $7-10

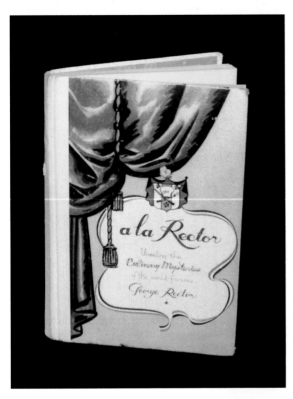

A La Rector cookbook signed by the author, George Rector. 1933. $45-55

Pyrex cookbook. 1953. $18-22

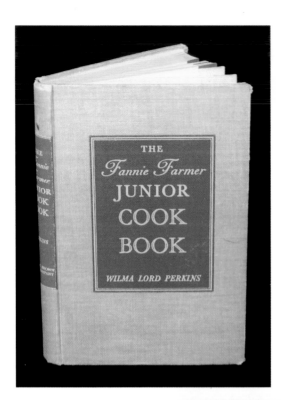

Fannie Farmer Junior Cook Book.
1945. $30-40

The Mixer, Hand Mixer and
Blender Cookbook. 1954. $15-20

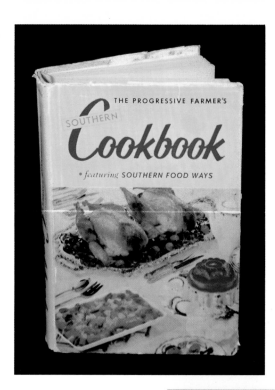

Southern Cookbook. 1961. $9-14

First Ladies Cook Book.
1982. $15-20

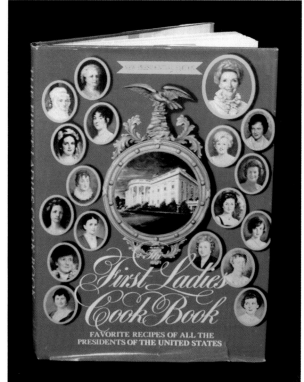

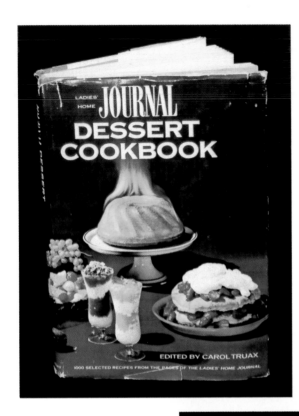

Ladies' Home Journal Dessert Cookbook. 1964. $9-12

American Family Cookbook. 1971. $10-15

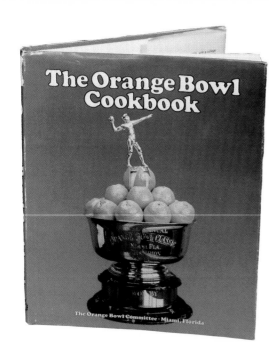

The Orange Bowl Cookbook.
1983. $10-15

Metal recipe boxes. 1950s-60s. $7-10 each

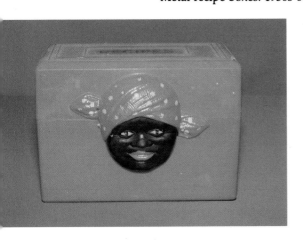

Aunt Jemima recipe box by Fosta.
1950s. $200-250

Metal recipe box advertising Bisquick. 1960s. $8-12

Wooden recipe box by Weis with recipes. 1950s. $12-15

Metal recipe box by Meta. 1950s.
$6-8

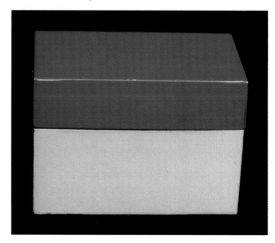

Plastic American Family Scale. 1960s. $15-20

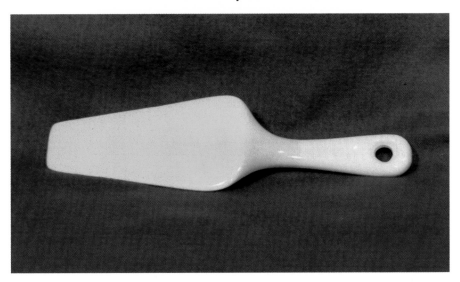

Glass pie lifter/cake server. 1940s-50s. $7-10

Ceramic pie lifter. 1950s. $20-30

Ceramic spoon rest. 1950s. $6-8

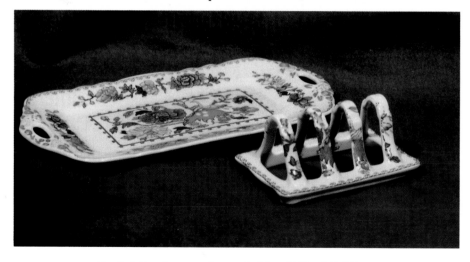

English floral tray and toast holder. 1940s. $70-100 set

Tin coasters set in plastic holder. 1950s. $5-7

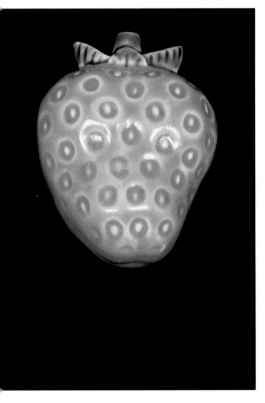

Ceramic strawberry wall pocket. "Japan." 1950s. $20-25

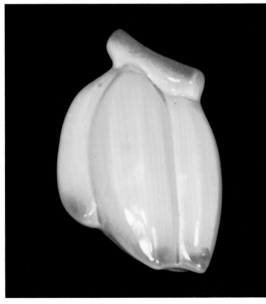

Ceramic banana wall pocket. "Japan." 1950s. $20-25

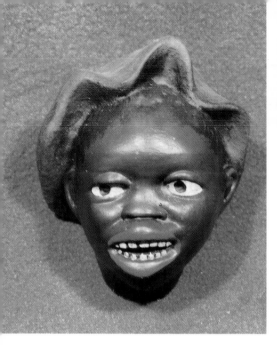

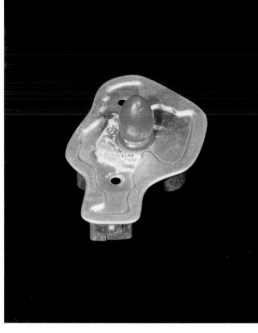

Chalk match holder. Jonny Griffin. 1940s. $85-100

Aluminum Santa cookie cutter with wood handle. 1940s. $5-7

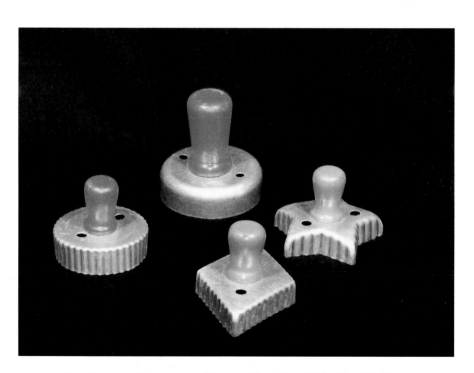

Aluminum cookie cutters with wood handles. 1940s-50s. $20-25 set

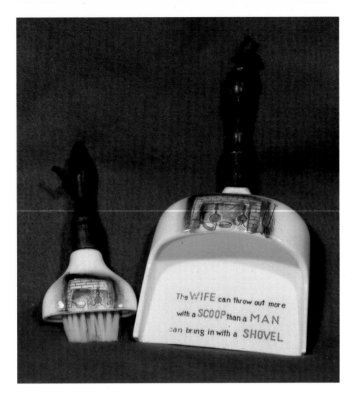

Ceramic crumb tray and brush. 1950s. $7-10

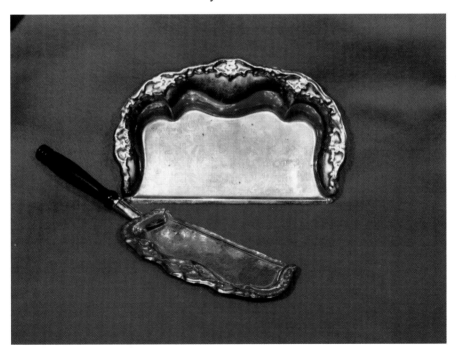

Silver crumb tray. 1940s. $10-15

Tin silent butler. 1940s. $20-25

Metal napkin holder. 1960s. $6-10

Metal napkin holder with
fruit decal. 1940s. $10-15

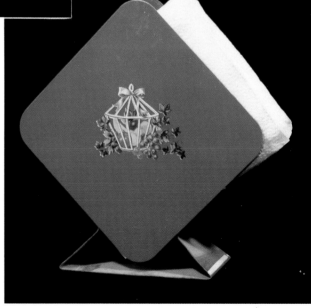

Ceramic cheese dish with mouse coming out the top. 1960s. $12-15

Pottery water jug. 1920s-30s. $25-35

"Hall" pottery creamer. 1940s. $10-15

Canning crock with handle.
1930s-40s. $30-40

Ceramic coffee cup reading
"Relax with coffee and a cigarette."
1950s-60s. $6-10

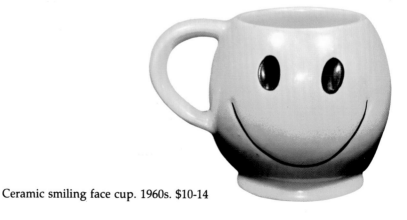

Ceramic smiling face cup. 1960s. $10-14

Happy face china cookie jar. 1960s. $65-75

Glass cookie jar. 1940s. $30-40

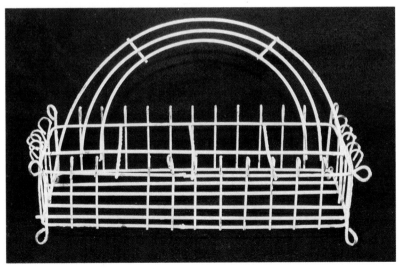

Plastic on metal drinking glass carrier. 1940s. $9-12

Bibliography

Franklin, Linda Campbell. *300 Years of Kitchen Collectibles.* Florence, Alabama: Americana Incorporated, 1981.

Collectors News. Grundy, Iowa. December, 1993.

The Antique Trader Weekly. Dubuque, Iowa. February 14, 1996.

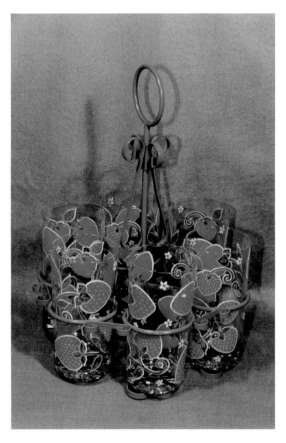

Embossed strawberries painted on six-piece glass set in wire holder. 1950s. $35-45